GIANT SQUID
Monsters of the Deep

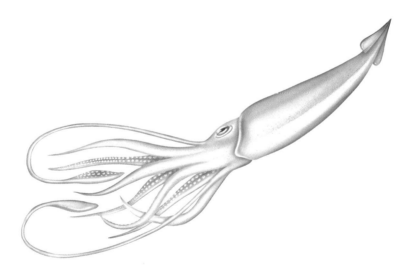

by Eulalia García
Illustrated by Gabriel Casadevall and Ali Garousi

Gareth Stevens Publishing
MILWAUKEE

7409311

For a free color catalog describing Gareth Stevens' list of high-quality books and multimedia programs, call 1-800-542-2595 (USA) or 1-800-461-9120 (Canada). Gareth Stevens Publishing's Fax: (414) 225-0377.
See our catalog, too, on the World Wide Web: http://gsinc.com

The editor would like to extend special thanks to Jan W. Rafert, Curator of Primates and Small Mammals, Milwaukee County Zoo, Milwaukee, Wisconsin, for his kind and professional help with the information in this book.

Library of Congress Cataloging-in-Publication Data

García, Eulalia.
    [Calamar gigante. English]
    Giant squid : monsters of the deep / by Eulalia García ; illustrated by Gabriel Casadevall and Ali Garousi.
        p. cm. – (Secrets of the animal world)
    Includes bibliographical references and index.
    Summary: Describes the physical characteristics, habitat, behavior, and life cycle of these immense marine predators.
    ISBN 0-8368-1644-7 (lib. bdg.)
    1. Giant squid–Juvenile literature. [1. Giant squid. 2. Squid.] I. Casadevall, Gabriel, ill. II. Garousi, Ali, ill. III. Title. IV. Series.
    QL430.3.A73G3713 1997
    594'.58–dc21   96-46915

This North American edition first published in 1997 by
Gareth Stevens Publishing
1555 North RiverCenter Drive, Suite 201
Milwaukee, Wisconsin 53212 USA

This U.S. edition © 1997 by Gareth Stevens, Inc. Created with original © 1993 Ediciones Este, S.A., Barcelona, Spain. Additional end matter © 1997 by Gareth Stevens, Inc.

Series editor: Patricia Lantier-Sampon
Editorial assistants: Diane Laska, Rita Reitci

Printed in the United States of America

1 2 3 4 5 6 7 8 9 01 00 99 98 97

CONTENTS

GIANTS FROM THE DEEP

Where giant squid live

At one time, giant squid were not thought of as real animals. They were regarded only as the subjects of sailors' tall tales. Then, in 1861, the first giant cephalopod was sighted. Everything scientists know now about the giant squid comes from those that have been found dead on the coast, captured, or pulled away from their enemies, the sperm whales.

Experts believe giant squid live between 1,640 and 4,900 feet (500 and 1,500 meters) deep in both the Atlantic and the Pacific oceans. The largest squid ever found measured 65 feet (20 m) in length with the tentacles extended and weighed 880 pounds (400 kilograms).

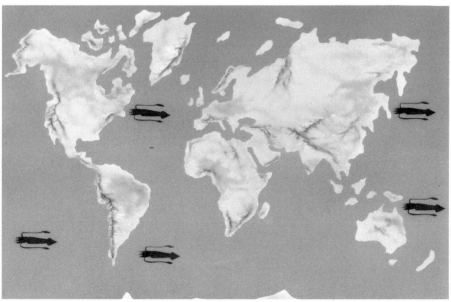

Giant squid have been seen in their habitat only a few times. The small squid in the photograph above live in shallow waters.

Giant squid live in deep waters. They may exist in all of Earth's oceans and seas.

The marine desert

Deserts are some of the poorest regions on Earth for plant and animal life because of lack of water. The sea also has deserts. In the abyssal plain, life is scarce due to lack of nourishment.

Marine life abounds in the upper waters, but beyond the continental shelf, where the sea descends to 20,000 feet (6,000 m) — the abyssal region — animals are less abundant.

The ocean bottom is Earth's largest habitat, a place with darkness, low temperatures, and enormous water pressure.

Beyond the continental shelf the ocean's floor plunges to 20,000 feet (6,000 m).

No human has ever walked on the ocean's floor. Only a small part of this enormous abyss has been explored.

In some places, the oceanic trenches are up to 36,000 feet (11,000 m) deep.

CONTINENTAL SHELF

ABYSSAL PLAIN

OCEANIC TRENCH

SEAMOUNTS

Life in the depths

The ocean's many inhabitants live at various levels of the immense mass of water that extends from the surface to the bottom. Some animals stay only in certain depths; others move between different layers, depending on their food needs.

The microscopic organisms that make up plankton live at 0-500 feet (0-150 m). Snipe eels and gulper eels live between 500 and 3,280 feet (150 and 1,000 m). Human eyes cannot perceive light at these depths. Snipe eels, with their large, scissorlike jaws, feed on abyssal shrimp. Some types of gulper eels can swallow prey larger than themselves.

Only a few species of animals live from 3,280 feet (1,000 m) to

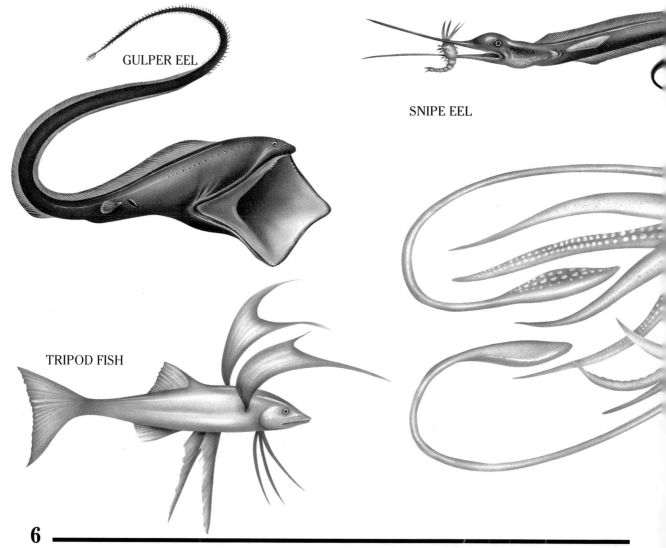

GULPER EEL

SNIPE EEL

TRIPOD FISH

the bottom of the ocean. Lack of competition is probably the main reason the creatures that live here are very large in size and few in number. These animals include the giant squid, which sperm whales descend to capture.

At the bottom of the ocean, animal life is represented by some fish, worms, anemones, sponges, and sea cucumbers. One unusual fish, called the tripod fish, settles on the ocean floor with its large fins to hunt for possible prey.

Many of the strangest animals that live in the deep are known only because they have been captured in nets.

ABYSSAL ANEMONE

GIANT SQUID

INSIDE THE GIANT SQUID

Giant squid belong to the mollusk phylum. Most mollusks are aquatic and marine, but some live on land, such as slugs and snails. The main characteristic of most mollusks is their shell, but in some it is internal, like the squid, or does not exist.

INK SAC
When the squid feels that it is in danger, it shoots a cloud of black ink from its anus; this disorients its enemy. The ink of some squid that live in very dark waters is luminous, so as to blind its predators and escape without being seen.

EYES
The giant squid has the largest eyes of any animal on Earth. They can measure 10 inches (25 centimeters) in diameter — bigger than a car's head-lights. They do not have a cornea but are still the most evolved eyes of all the invertebrates.

PEN
Forms the squid's skeleton. It serves as a rod to maintain the squid's long shape. It also supports the muscles.

FINS
Triangular fins at the end of the squid's body are very flexible. They act as stabilizers when the squid swims and help it change direction.

DIGESTIVE GLAND

INTESTINE

STOMACH

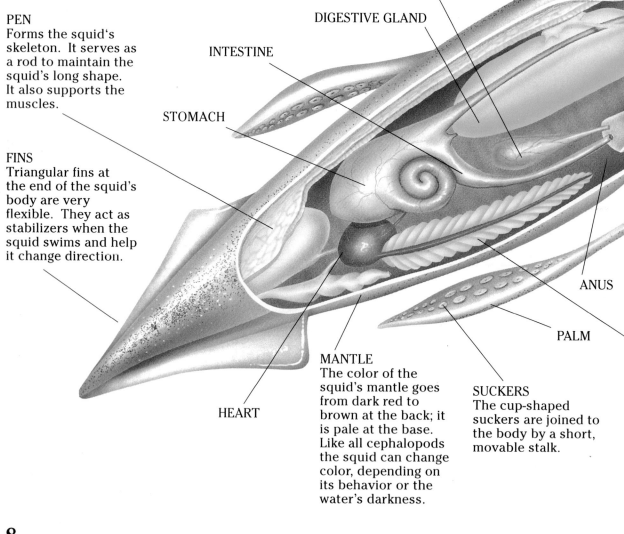

ANUS

PALM

MANTLE
The color of the squid's mantle goes from dark red to brown at the back; it is pale at the base. Like all cephalopods the squid can change color, depending on its behavior or the water's darkness.

SUCKERS
The cup-shaped suckers are joined to the body by a short, movable stalk.

HEART

HEAD
The giant squid's head can be 3 feet (1 m) long. The mouth is inside, surrounded by eight thick arms and two thinner tentacles, which it uses to capture prey.

BRAIN

PARROT BEAK
The giant squid's jaws are similar to a parrot's beak. The top jaw is pointed, and, together with the lower one, forms a sharp area that cuts like a knife.

ESOPHAGUS

ARMS
The arms are much shorter than the tentacles. Each arm has two lines of suckers that become smaller toward the end. Males have two modified arms for mating.

SIPHON
A tube the squid uses in propulsion. When it expels water through the tube, the squid moves in the opposite direction.

RADULA
Like a file, the radula is a rasping tongue. It has rows of horny teeth. After food is reduced to bits in the beak, it is pushed into the gullet with the radula.

TENTACLES
The two large tentacles function like tweezers when the squid captures its prey. Each tentacle has a wider area, the palm, that has vents and small, adhesive bulges.

GILLS
The squid breathes through two large comb-like gills. The water surrounding these gills constantly goes in and out of the mantle cavity with the squid's muscle movements.

Besides being a mollusk, the giant squid is a cephalopod, a word that means "feet in the head." It is the most agile and movable mollusk in existence.

GIANT SQUID HABITAT

Between two waters

Some marine animals can stay at a certain level because their density is the same as the water around them, or because they have mechanisms that suspend them for a long time. Without these mechanisms, the animals would be too heavy, and they would sink.

The heavy giant squid would sink to the bottom if it were not constantly adjusting its buoyancy. To balance its enormous weight without swimming, it has developed a special mechanism. It has particles called ammonium

Giant squid remain at a given level when their density is equal to that of the water surrounding them.

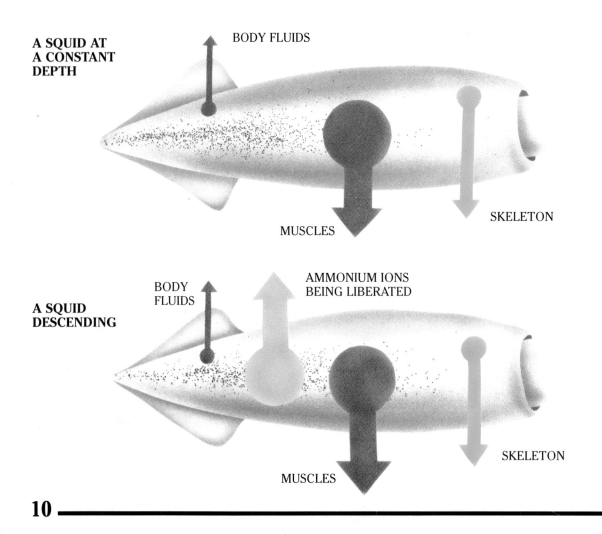

A SQUID AT A CONSTANT DEPTH

BODY FLUIDS

MUSCLES

SKELETON

A SQUID DESCENDING

BODY FLUIDS

AMMONIUM IONS BEING LIBERATED

MUSCLES

SKELETON

One crustacean lives suspended with the help of its long legs and antennae. The other does not need these appendages to live on the sea floor.

ions in its muscles that give it lightness. The giant squid can either keep or get rid of the ammonium ions.

To descend, the giant squid frees the ions to make itself heavier. To ascend or maintain a level, it keeps the ions to make itself lighter.

Giant squid also maintain their position through organs called statocysts. These small, slow-growing organs develop at a 45° angle. Because of this, scientists think giant squid float in a slightly inclined position.

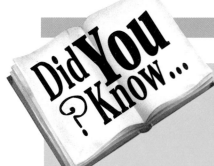
that there are flying squid?

Most ocean squid are fast swimmers. Through jet propulsion, which other cephalopods like the octopus also use, squid cross the seas like living torpedoes. Some squid seem to fly outside of the water. They propel themselves so swiftly that they scoot along the water's surface like arrows.

Hunters of the deep

Giant squid are predators of a spectacular size. The third longest animal in the sea is the giant squid.

Some scientists believe the giant squid is a scavenger that cannot capture live prey. However, remains of ocean squid have been found in some

These are the giant squid's suckers, capable of immobilizing prey or leaving deep scars.

Fearsome sharks have many enemies — humans, killer whales, dolphins, and the terrifying giant squid.

giant squid stomachs. To trap its prey, the giant squid moves forward, expelling water through the siphon and stretching its tentacles. These tentacles have suckers with hooks, and any effort to escape is useless.

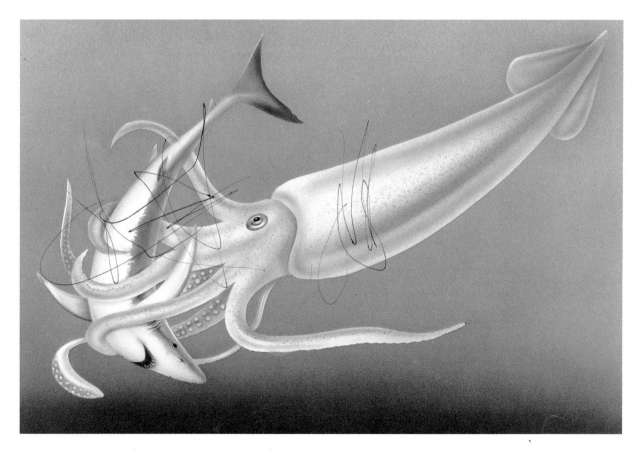

COLOSSUS OF THE DEPTHS

The importance of the giant squid

Because of the giant squid's large size and highly developed structure, scientists study its nervous system to find out more about our own.

The giant squid is also an important link in the feeding chain of the sea. The chain starts with the sperm whale, which feeds on schools of ocean squid and on many specimens of giant squid. Squid feed on fish, which feed on animal micro-organisms. The microorganisms feed on microplankton.

See how small a human is beside the colossal animals that exist or have existed on Earth.

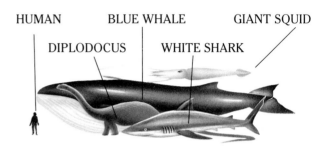

HUMAN   BLUE WHALE   GIANT SQUID

DIPLODOCUS   WHITE SHARK

This is the sperm whale feeding chain, in which the giant squid is the second link.

that oases exist at the bottom of the sea?

Oases exist not only in Earth's deserts; they also occur in marine depths. In the deepest oceans, there is no plant life to carry out photosynthesis because of the lack of light. But in some places 7,875 feet (2,400 m) deep, bacteria take the place of plants as producers of organic material. These bacteria feed on hydrogen sulfide. Numerous animals, from giant tube worms to crabs to fish, gather to feed in these oases.

The giant squid's neighbors

The part of the sea where the giant squid lives lies between the upper waters and the darkest depths. This region is inhabited by other animals that are also predators. These creatures look strange and have unusual names, such as hatchet fish, knifefish, dragonfish, viper-fish, and sea devils.

Toward the bottom, animals become scavengers as well as predators because they have few prey to hunt. Scavengers eat the corpses of other animals, which descend to the bottom when they die. The predators usually look fierce, with their

The devilfish has a mouth that opens very wide. It seems to be joined to the body by a spring. Its powerful teeth are like bars, so prey cannot escape.

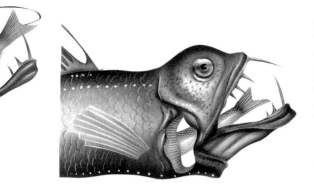

huge mouths and stomachs. Any prey that shows up will probably not escape, no matter how large it is.

Usually, the metabolism of animals that live in the depths is slower than those inhabiting the surface. They have undeveloped hearts, kidneys, and brains, as well as small eyes and weak muscles. This is why they are not very active. The giant squid meets other cephalopods during its ocean trips, such as the blind octopus or transparent squid that look like jellyfish.

This squid's body is transparent, so its internal organs are obvious.

This creature is a sea devil. Its upper lip is curled, so its teeth are pointing outward.

CEPHALOPOD EVOLUTION

Origin of life in the depths

Many animal families existing on Earth's surface are represented in the far reaches of the sea. So why did some animals begin to colonize such dark, barren regions? There are two theories to explain this.

The first theory states that some animals once lived close to the water's surface. These animals moved deeper as the pressure caused by physical changes became greater over time.

The second theory states that some animals had adapted to

living in very cold seas. When the water temperature began to increase, they had to move to colder, deeper water. All the animals in the depths have relatives on the surface.

Cephalopods are well represented in the deep by octopuses and squid, whose origins date back about 200 million years. But other

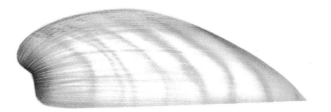

Scientists thought these primitive one-valved mollusks were extinct until living species were discovered in the ocean depths.

cephalopods appeared before these early animals — the nautiloids. Only one nautiloid species survives today, the nautilus. The ammonites, now extinct, had shells as large as 3 feet (1 m) in diameter.

For 45 million years, many cephalopods lived in the primitive seas.

The first cephalopods had external shells like this nautilus, the only survivor of the nautiloid group.

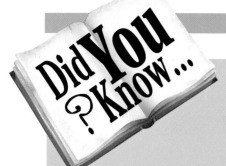

that there are
luminous squid?

The darkness of the oceanic depths is broken only by the light that many animals produce through their photophores. These animals include jellyfish, squid, sharks, marine prawns, and many fish. Some fish use the light as a lure for capturing prey. Some can imitate the sparkles of light produced by fish of another species. The light can also serve as camouflage.

GIANT SQUID BEHAVIOR

Number one enemy

The giant squid has few enemies. The most fearsome is the sperm whale, which considers the squid its favorite meal. The squid has good vision for sighting its predators in order to avoid them. Still, it is often attacked by the sperm whale. The squid uses its incredible arms in a battle to drown the whale, which needs to breathe air. The squid fastens its suckers and powerful hooks on the sperm whale's skin. Scars from the giant squid's

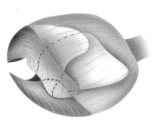

The jaws of the giant squid look like this. The squid chews prey with its parrot beak before swallowing.

suckers are often found close to the mouth and the head of sperm whales. These are the tracks left by the battles with these sea giants.

The sperm whale and the giant squid are enemies. They often engage in fierce battles, and it is usually survival of the fittest.

Reproduction

Scientists do not know much about how the giant squid reproduce. They may mate by intertwining their arms. Two of the male's arms are used to carry sperm to the female.

The females have glands called nidationaries, which produce a gelatin in which to wrap their eggs.

Two of the male giant squid's arms, called hectocotyles, transfer sperm to the female.

The male also packs its sperm in gelatin, forming spermatophores that measure 8 inches (20 cm) long.

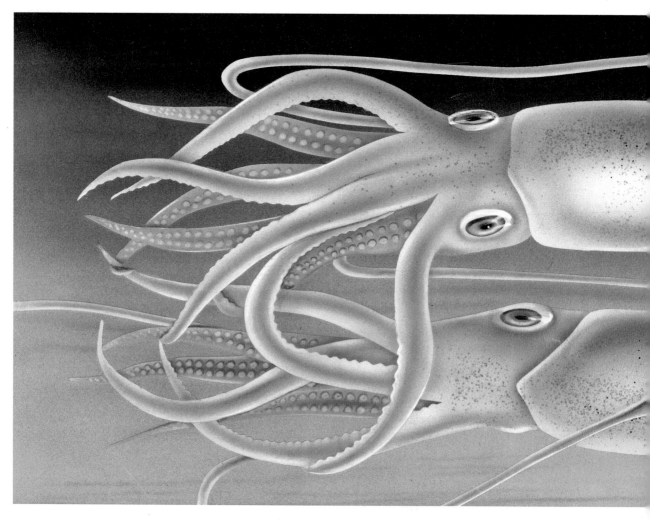

With its hectocotyles, the male squid gathers sperm from its circular cleft and transfers it to the female. The females then lay a huge amount of very small, white eggs.

The giant squid probably abandon the eggs in the gelatin masses, which then float around in the water. Of all the mollusks, cephalopods are the only ones that do not have a larval phase in their development. Instead, they have what is called direct development. Small cephalopods that look similar to the adults emerge from the eggs.

A baby ocean squid is still joined to the egg from which it feeds.

A hug may be part of the mating ritual for the giant squid.

APPENDIX TO

GIANT SQUID
Monsters of the Deep

GIANT SQUID SECRETS

Slow, but long-lived. Abyssal animals have a slower growth rate than their relatives in the upper layers, but they live longer. Some mollusks live as long as one hundred years.

▼ **The marvelous lamp.** One species of abyssal squid has

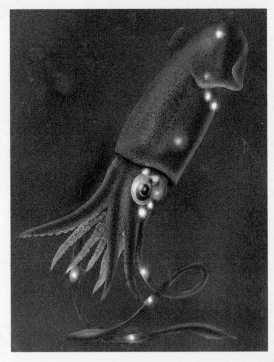

an astonishing feature. In spite of its small size, it can display a set of twenty-four different-colored lights.

▼ **Bulgy eyes.** The common hatchet fish has a hatchet shape, silver coloring, and enormous eyes that look up.

▼ **Strange young.** Dragonfish larvae have long stalks with eyes at the end. In time, the stalks shorten until the eyes rest within the orbits.

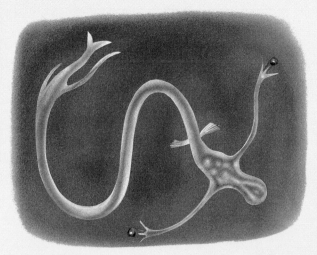

▶ **Diver's sickness.** Deep sea divers who ascend too quickly after diving in deep waters can suffer the bends. A sudden change in pressure causes small bubbles of nitrogen to form on tissues. This causes vomiting, great body pain, and sometimes even death.

Pen and ink. The squid has a pen as its skeleton, as well as ink, so it was given the ancient name of the quill pen and inkwell — *calamario.*

1. Does the giant squid have a skeleton?
a) Yes, it is internal, and it is called a pen.
b) No. It is the same as an octopus.
c) Yes. It has an external shell, like other mollusks.

2. Where do giant squid lay eggs?
a) They carry them on their body.
b) They deposit them on the ocean floor.
c) They let them drift in the sea.

3. Giant squid are:
a) crustaceans.
b) mammals.
c) cephalopod mollusks.

4. The giant squid's main enemy is:
a) the white shark.
b) the sperm whale.
c) humans.

5. Which animals are not represented in the abyss?
a) Dragonfish.
b) Birds.
c) Sea devils.

6. Giant squid live:
a) between 1,640 to 4,900 feet (500 to 1,500 m) deep.
b) at 36,100 feet (11,000 m) deep.
c) near the water's surface.

The answers to GIANT SQUID SECRETS questions are on page 32.

GLOSSARY

abundant: plentiful; having a large amount of.

abyss: a limitless area or space.

abyssal plain: any of the huge, flat areas of the ocean floor.

adapt: to make changes or adjustments in order to survive in a changing environment.

agile: nimble; able to move quickly or easily.

amphibians: cold-blooded animals that live both in water and on land. Frogs, toads, and salamanders are amphibians.

anemones: invertebrate animals that live in the ocean. Sea anemones usually attach themselves to rocks and shells and feed on plankton that they catch with their tentacles.

appendage: a body part that is attached to the main body, or trunk.

aquatic: of or relating to water; living or growing in water.

ascend: to move upward.

bacteria: tiny, single-celled organisms. Some bacteria help digest food; others can cause infections or illness.

camouflage: a way of disguising something or someone to make it look like its surroundings.

cephalopods: mollusks that have arms attached to their heads, such as squid and octopuses.

colonize: to set up a group or community.

continental shelf: a shallow submarine plain bordering a continent and ending in a steep slope to the oceanic abyss.

crustaceans: animals with segmented bodies and a hard outer shell that live mostly in water. Lobsters, shrimp, and crabs are crustaceans.

descend: to move in a downward direction.

evolution: the process of changing or developing gradually from one form to another. Over time, all living things evolve to survive changing environments, or they may become extinct.

expel: to push out or get rid of.

extinct: no longer in existence.

fins: thin, flat parts that stick out from the body of a water animal. Fins are used by the animal for steering and balance.

gills: the breathing organs in all fish and many invertebrates that take oxygen from water; also known as the branchiae.

gullet: throat or esophagus of an animal.

habitat: the natural home of a plant or animal.

immense: huge; of great size.

internal: located within or inside something.

invertebrates: any animals that do not have a spinal column, or backbone.

ion: atom or group of atoms that carries a positive or negative electrical charge.

larva (*pl.* larvae): in the life cycle of insects, amphibians, fish, and some other organisms, the stage that comes after the egg but before full development.

mammals: warm-blooded animals that have backbones and hair, and give birth to living young. Female mammals produce milk to feed their young.

marine: of or related to the sea.

mate (*v*): to join together (animals) to produce young.

metabolism: the changes that occur in body cells to process new materials entering the body and to produce energy.

microscopic: capable of being seen only with the help of a microscope.

mollusks: invertebrate animals, such as snails and clams, that usually live in water and have hard outer shells.

nautiloid: a shell-bearing cephalopod.

photophores: organs that emit light; luminous spots that occur on some marine animals.

photosynthesis: the process by which the energy of sunlight is converted by plants into food, using chlorophyll and carbon dioxide.

plankton: tiny plants and animals that drift in the ocean.

predators: animals that kill and eat other animals.

prey: animals that are hunted for food by other animals.

primitive: of or relating to an early and usually simple stage of development. Nautiloids were primitive cephalopods.

scavengers: animals that feed on dead animals and plants.

species: animals or plants that are closely related and often similar in behavior and appearance. Members of the same species can breed together.

sperm: male reproductive cell.

statocysts: organs of equilibrium, or balance, that giant squid use to maintain position.

tentacles: long, narrow, flexible parts or limbs that certain animals use for moving around and catching prey.

ACTIVITIES

◆ Although they look different, the octopus and the squid are closely related. Using facts from books or from a visit to a natural history museum, compare these two animals. In how many ways are they physically similar? How are they different? Compare their eating habits and behavior in nature. Do they capture and eat the same kinds of foods? How does each behave when danger threatens? Do you think the giant squid has the same kind of habits that the smaller ocean squid has? Think of ways that they are the same and different.

◆ There are many legends about sea monsters in all parts of the world. Look up some of these legends and compare the descriptions of the monsters with what you know about the giant squid. Think about the giant squid's long arms and tentacles, about its big eyes and huge body. Do you think some of these sea monster legends could be explained as rare sightings of the giant squid? Could remains of the giant squid washed up on shore have caused some of these stories?

MORE BOOKS TO READ

Colors of the Sea (series). E. Ethan and M. Bearanger (Gareth Stevens)
First Facts about Giant Sea Creatures. Gina Phillips (Kidsbooks)
Giants of the Deep. Q. L. Pearce (Lowell House)
Large Sea Creatures. Jason Cooper (Rourke Group)
The Man-of-War at Sea. D. Shale and J. Coldrey (Gareth Stevens)
Monster Myths: The Truth about Water Monsters. Staton Rabin (Watts)
Ocean Life. R. Morris (EDC)
Sea Life. (Educational Insights)
Stranger Than Fiction: Sea Monsters. Melvin Berger (Avon)
Tentacles: Octopus, Squid, and Their Relatives. James Martin
    (Crown Books)
Under the Sea from A to Z. Anne Doubilet (Crown Books)

VIDEOS

Ocean Animals. (Agency for Instructional Technology)
The Octopus. (Barr Films)
Sea Wonders. (Society for Visual Educational)
World Beneath the Sea. (Video Dimension)

PLACES TO VISIT

Monterey Bay Aquarium
886 Cannery Row
Monterey, CA 93940

**Vancouver Public
    Aquarium**
Stanley Park
Vancouver, BC V6B 3X8

Sydney Aquarium
Wheat Road, Pier 26
Sydney, NSW, Australia

**Kelly Tarlton's
    Underwater World**
Orakei Wharf
Tamaki Drive
Auckland 1, New Zealand

Aquarium du Quebec
1675 Avenue des Hotels
Sainte-Foy, Quebec
G1W 4S3

**Aquarium of the
    Americas**
No. 1 Canal Street
New Orleans, LA 70130

National Aquarium
Lady Denman Drive
Canberra, NSW, Australia

INDEX

Answers to GIANT SQUID SECRETS questions:
1. **a**
2. **c**
3. **c**
4. **b**
5. **b**
6. **a**